The New Women Included

THE NEW WOMEN INCLUDED

A Book of Services and Prayers

THE St HILDA COMMUNITY
With new introductions and prayers

In loving memory of Brother Thaddaeus SSF
who was a good friend to the St Hilda Community.

First published in Great Britain
1991
Revised and updated edition 1996
SPCK
Holy Trinity Church
Marylebone Road
London NW1 4DU

British Library Cataloguing in
Publication Data
The New Women Included.
1. Christianity. Women
I. St Hilda Community
262.15

ISBN 0–281–04950–5

Printed in Great Britain by
Redwood Books, Trowbridge
Typeset by The Midlands Book
Typesetting Co. Loughborough

Contents

Acknowledgements

The St Hilda Community would like to thank the following for permission to reproduce copyright material:

The Congregation of Abraxas, First Unitarian Church of Berkeley CA, for 'The feast is ended, depart in peace'.

David Adam for 'Glory in all my seeing', 'From the flowing of the tide to its ebbing' and 'God of love and tenderness' from *Tides and Seasons* (Triangle/SPCK 1989).

Ann Peart for 'Today we share bread and wine together' and 'Let us give thanks'.

The Ashram Community Trust for 'I light the candle, the light shines out' and 'As women break bread' from *Community Worship* (Ashram Community Trust).

Rachel Carr and Margaret Orr Deas for the St Hilda's Day liturgy.

Jim Cotter for 'Be in love with life' and 'The blessing of God' from *Prayer at Night* (Cairns Publications, 4th edition, 1988), 'O God I seek you while you may be found' from *Prayer in the Morning* (Cairns Publications, 2nd edition, 1990) and 'Beloved, our Father and Mother' from *Healing — more or less* (Cairns Publications 1987).

Darton Longman and Todd for 'Peace and love are always alive in us' from *Enfolded in Love: Daily Readings with Julian of Norwich* (Darton Longman and Todd 1980).

Brenda Denvir for 'We believe in the presence of God in the world'.

F. Gerald Downing for 'Rage, Wisdom, and our lives inflame' (*Chrysalis*, MOW, June 1987).

Erica Dunmow for 'Sisters and brothers of the Community of St Hilda'.

Christine Eilbeck for 'We are the meeting place of heaven and earth' and 'We confess our failure'.

Monica Furlong for 'We adore the glory and the truth that is God', 'Jesus, who was lost and found in the garden', 'O God, we bring you our failure', 'We hold up our smallness to your greatness', 'God, who cares for us', 'O God, our Father and Mother' and 'Those who work for change suffer resistance'.

Monica Furlong for 'O God who gives all that is good', 'God our father and our mother', 'In friendship, love, warmth and laughter', 'I open this season of Advent', 'Let us be a light', 'We stand at the turning of the year', 'May the spirit of Jesus be born in us', 'Today we share bread and wine', 'We seek to be transformed', 'May the star', 'We need time', 'Lent is a time', 'We worship the God', 'The holiness of the dove', and for the Easter liturgy.

Edwina Gateley for 'Be silent, Be still' and 'Into your hands, Lord' from *Psalms of a Laywoman* (Claretian Publications 1981).

Mildred Graham for 'O God, gentle and generous'.

Beth Hamilton for 'Once upon a time' from 'The Journey' (included in *Womanguides*, ed. Rosemary Radford Ruether, Beacon Press, Boston, 1985).

Carter Heyward for 'In the beginning was God'.

Lillalou Hughes for compiling 'The bread we bring'.

The Iona Community for 'The Drama of Creation' and 'The Drama of the Incarnation'.

Keith Jenkins for 'Today we share bread and wine together' and 'Let us give thanks'.

Peter Kettle for 'This, the springtime of the year', the second verse of 'Be gentle when you touch bread' and 'Broken for us'.

Ann Lewin for 'Flame-dancing Spirit' from *By the Way* (1990).

Lillenas Publishing Company/Thankyou Music for 'You shall go out with joy' by Stuart Dauermann © 1975.

George MacLeod for 'Let thy Resurrection light radiate all our worship' from *The Whole Earth Shall Cry Glory* (Wild Goose Publications 1985).

Adrian Mitchell for 'Final Chant' from *For Beauty Douglas – Collected Poems 1953–79* (Allison and Busby 1982). Neither 'Final Chant' nor any other work by Adrian Mitchell is to be used in connection with any examination whatsoever.

Janet Morley for 'God our vision', 'O God our deliverer you cast down the mighty', 'Christ our healer', 'Spirit of integrity', 'Spirit of truth whom the world can never grasp', 'God our deliverer, whose approaching birth', 'God our mother', 'O God, the power of the powerless', 'For the darkness of waiting', 'May the God who dances in creation', 'Blessed is our brother Jesus' and 'May Holy Wisdom' from *All Desires Known* (WIT/MOW 1988) and also for 'God of the outsider'.

Priscilla Morton for 'We have come together', 'Dear God', and 'As we have shared our hopes'.

Margaret Orr Deas for 'Forgiving and understanding God', 'Loving and all-knowing God' and 'For moments of laughter'.

The NCCC, USA, for 'Keeper and Companion of us all' from the study on 'The Community of Women and Men in the Church' and Commission on Faith and Order (included in *No Longer Strangers*, WCC Publications 1983).

The National Christian Education Council for 'We do not understand, eternal God' from *Prayers for the Church Community* compiled by Roy Chapman and Donald Hilton (NCEC).

Oxford Women's Liturgy for 'God of justice and peace, you stand with those who are poor'.

R. G. Parsons c/o the Canterbury Press for 'O living bread from heaven'.

Penguin Books for an extract from *Bede: A History of the English Church and People*, trans. Leo Sherley-Price, © 1955, 1968 (Penguin Classics, revised edition, 1968).

Elizabeth Rice for 'The living God, the living, moving Spirit of God' (included in *No Longer Strangers*, WCC Publications 1983).

Nicola Slee for 'We believe in God — Maker, Redeemer and Sustainer of Life'.

Ateliers et Presses de Taizé for 'Ubi caritas et amor', 'Jubilate Deo', 'O Lord, hear my prayer' and 'Bless the Lord, my soul'.

Elsa Tamez for 'Come let us celebrate the supper of Jesus'.

Commission on Common Worship, Unitarian Universalist Association for 'From the fragmented world of our everyday lives' (included in *Leading Congregations in Worship — A Guide*).

Rachel C. Wahlberg for 'We believe in God who created women and men' (included in *No Longer Strangers*, WCC Publications 1983).

Judith Walker-Riggs for 'May the power and the mystery go before us' (included in *Echoes*, Unitarian Worship Sub-committee 1982).

Liz Waller for 'Glory be to you, Ground of all Being' and 'I deny God's gifts in me'.

Pat Willmitt for 'We need your forgiveness, merciful God'.

Lois M. Wilson for 'The blessing of the God of Sarah and Hagar, as of Abraham'.

Lala Winkley for 'God, lover of us all, most holy one'.

Miriam Therese Winter for 'In the beginning, in the very beginning' and 'I will pour clean water upon you' from *WomanPrayer, WomanSong* (Meyer-Stone Books).

and from traditional sources:
'Thanks be to God that we have risen this day' (Alexander Carmichael, *Carmina Gadelica*), and 'Now may every living being' (Sakyamuni Buddha).

The Community has made every effort to identify copyright holders and to obtain their permission, but would be glad to hear of any inadvertent errors or omissions.

Part One

The life of Christ's servant Abbess Hilda, whom all her acquaintance called Mother because of her wonderful devotion and grace . . . was the fulfilment of a dream which her mother had when Hilda was an infant, during the time that her husband was living in banishment, where he died of poison. In this dream she fancied that he was suddenly taken away, and although she searched everywhere she could find no trace of him. When all her efforts had failed, she discovered a most valuable jewel under her garments; and as she looked closely, it emitted such a brilliant light that all Britain was lit by its splendour. This dream was fulfilled in her daughter, whose life afforded a shining example not only to herself but to all who wished to live a good life. . . .

Bede, *A History of the English Church and People.*

O GOD our vision,
in our mother's womb
you formed us for your glory.
As your servant Hilda
shone like a jewel in the church
may we now delight to claim her gifts
of judgement and inspiration
reflected in the women of this age,
through Jesus Christ, Amen.

Collect for St Hilda's Day
(November 17)

Introduction: St Hilda's Now *Monica Furlong*

We asked our members to answer three questions – what brought them to St Hilda's in the first place, what they liked about it and what they didn't like. On this page, and elsewhere in the book, you will find their answers:

What I like about it, I suppose is that um . . . it's kind of very real – it's more what I imagine the early church would have been like, a small community of people. It's not governed by any kind of hierarchy or predictable order of things, it comes from the heart. . . .

I was told by a woman friend about a group that was having a non-sexist liturgy, and I came along and found that not only was it non-sexist but there seemed to be a different atmosphere about the thing altogether. I've been coming for the past three years. It's had its ups and downs because people are only human – they're not perfect – but there's a kind of spark of life and hope about it somehow. . . .

THE ST HILDA Community was founded in February, 1987, with two intentions. One was to encourage women and men to worship together in a way much more inclusive of women than was, or is, usual in the churches. The other intention was to invite women ordained abroad to celebrate in Britain, partly as a form of recognition of women's priesthood and partly to offer people in Britain an experience of women's ministry at the altar. (This was in opposition to a decision arrived at by the General Synod of the Church of England the previous July refusing to allow women 'lawfully ordained abroad' to celebrate the Eucharist in Britain. We believed this to be grossly unjust to the women, as well as foolish at a time when the Church of England was seriously considering ordaining women.)

So it was that a group of us assembled in St Benet's, the chapel of Queen Mary College, in London's East End, and slowly worked out a ground plan for this new liturgical group. At first our liturgies were carbon copies of the church services many of us had known, with people reading from lecterns, using the Alternative Service Book for most of the words, and preaching sermons. Gradually the formality relaxed into a more intimate style; we had much the same liturgical purpose as the churches, but the stiffness, and the dull language of the ASB, almost immediately began to seem entirely inappropriate. We sat in a circle (some of us on the floor), we wrote our own prayers and liturgies (Janet Morley was the great inspiration), we used other materials – poems, newspaper cuttings – as well as the Bible, to focus our thinking, and nobody attempted to preach. We simply talked as a group about the Bible readings, sometimes in angry or derogatory terms.

Intercession usually consisted of members lighting a candle and mentioning a name or an issue. Singing and dancing became ways of deepening our prayer and our closeness to one another.

Of course, none of these things seem very new now – many other groups have used such techniques and we still use them ourselves – but for us at the time they felt very fresh. In particular our change of method led us past the passivity so many lay people experience in church, and forced us to think in detail about the shape and meaning of liturgy. It was remarkable to discover the sense of shyness and taboo many otherwise confident and articulate men and women had about finding words to utter the Christian mysteries, or leading others in doing so. There was a deep terror of 'getting it wrong'. It surprised us into an awareness of just how much clerical professionalism had disempowered laity. But it was lovely to see people, who at first found the idea of putting together a service too difficult to contemplate, suddenly finding they could do so, in some cases with extraordinary imagination and skill. (It was not unlike watching people who were quite sure that they 'could not dance' gradually coming to do so in a totally spontaneous way in the simple form of circle dancing we often used.) We began

We had a new woman deacon who was very keen on feminist theology and she dragged me along with her to St Hilda's so she had somebody to go with.

So what did you think of it when you got there?

I felt the building (St Benet's) was like going into a womb. It had a strong sense of female spirituality and a very strong emphasis on the importance of the feminine . . . it felt rather distant from East London. . . .

I enjoy the discussions and the freedom with which people are able to question or express their doubts and nobody, nobody is looked at as though they are less perfect as a Christian for having doubts; through expressing them people seem to come to a better understanding of what faith's about . . . being in company with people who have had the same experience of feeling oppressed and repressed in the church. Spontaneity. Emphasis not on doing things right or wrong, but on being.

to see that we were performing a healing function for ourselves and others – 'enabling' in the current jargon.

In this we were particularly lucky in having Suzanne Fageol as our priest – an American woman who had a flair for making liturgy come alive, but who held strongly to the idea that it was 'our' liturgy and not 'hers'. Suzanne celebrated on our first Easter – in the student common-room off the chapel at Queen Mary, since we had been asked not to use the chapel – and over one hundred people came. We kept a candle burning in the empty chapel – a sad symbol of a Church emptied of its real energy.

What made the Community different from other Christian feminist groups at the time was that, almost from the outset, and without apology, we were engaged in public controversy. We believed that what we were witnessing, by using women priests, and exploring new attitudes to gender, needed to be heard by the Church of England. It was. In October 1988 the then Bishop of London, Graham Leonard, had us evicted from the Queen Mary chapel, since we would not give up inviting women priests to celebrate the Eucharist. Queen Mary College itself had no objection to our presence; on the contrary they seemed rather proud of us, and in any case, since St Benet's was part of an ecumenical centre, it was common for Methodist women ministers to celebrate Communion there. However, the London diocese owned the land on which the chapel stood, and used this convenient fact to expel us, threatening legal sanctions. The Methodist/Anglican church of Holy Trinity, Bow, just down the road, immediately offered us hospitality (the land on which Holy Trinity stood was owned by the Methodists and therefore the bishop could not interfere).

The Community continued on its way, receiving many interesting visitors from overseas and from all over Britain who had heard of it and wanted to see for themselves. Numbers waxed after the eviction, which was a bit of a problem for a while – the intimacy that gave our liturgies particular poignancy tended to disappear when the group got very large. There was a strong disagreement within the Community about whether we were primarily about women priests, or, as seemed more and more to be the case, about lay participation. Some valued members left, but the rest of us continued. As time went on, however, a number of the keenest original members moved away, died (in one case), or felt that St Hilda's had served its turn. We noticed that all our most faithful members now came from outside the East End, and to serve their needs we founded another St Hilda's on the other side of London. For a while we kept both going simultaneously, but eventually it seemed better to consolidate in one place.

'West End' St Hilda's, which met at Notting Hill, was subtly different from its forebear. There were many more women than men (we had been used to an equal mix), and this was a disappointment to us since

A friend of mine saw an advertisement in the Church Times. *As a man I had been committed for a long time to women's ordination because I increasingly felt that women had much to offer which was being denied in the life of the church.*

So when you came what did you feel about it?

I found it a tremendously exciting event. It was the first Easter at St Hilda's and it said something that wasn't being said anywhere else in the church. . . .

I'm from an Irish Catholic background and I suppose I value very much the spontaneity and realness and I feel women can come here and be real. And also I like having men with us, and also the feeling that we can include people who may feel they don't belong anywhere. Coming here makes me feel I know who I am. . . .

Having lived in England a little over two years, I was looking out for groups, women's groups, where spirituality would be important and I heard about St Hilda's in my wanderings through Quaker groups and other groups, mostly of marginalized women. So I came along a couple of times and now I live a bit nearer I can come more often. . .

we were committed to the idea of sharing. Once a group has shaped itself in this way, it is quite difficult to change it, since a man who finds himself alone in the gathering can feel subtly uncomfortable (as women have so often done in all-male gatherings). But that apart the group was lively and creative. At first it met in a room in a church, but finding that rather formal, it began to alternate meetings between members' homes and Holy Trinity House, Orsett Terrace, Paddington, an Anglican Franciscan house. Under Brother Thaddaeus's leadership this house had a wonderfully warm and homely feel, and because we liked the kitchen there so much we formed the idea of making a meal the centre of our liturgy, as the early Christians seem to have done, and as practising Jews still do in their own homes.

Not all our liturgies took exactly the same form. In some we would begin the meal and then break if off in order to make intercession and pass round bread and wine. In others we would hold the service in an adjoining room and then come to the table immediately afterwards. In others again we would finish the meal and then consecrate the food and drink left on the table and pass it to one another. One of the things we were learning, as Rachel mentions in her contribution, is to work creatively within the framework of the liturgy. However carefully it was prepared, and it needed to be so – we did not countenance sloppiness – there was always room for a spontaneous word or action where it was appropriate – a joke, a remark, a gesture – as a response to events or needs which arose in the course of the evening. And for this to work we needed to be relaxed with one another, and acutely aware of the feeling of the gathering.

Setting the Eucharist in the context of a meal gradually became the outstanding feature of West End St Hilda's. We had always taken hospitality seriously, but now the meal took on a deeply sacramental quality, and, realizing this, members began to cook for it very lovingly and carefully.

Our members were, as they had been from the beginning, from mixed religious backgrounds, some churchgoers, or ex-churchgoers, some not sure if they were believers in God, though they tended to be seekers. St Hilda's has always included people, usually women, leaving the Christian churches in exasperation, but it is also true that a number of our members have made their way back into church involvement, either as well as, or instead of, their commitment to St Hilda's.

We saw, and see, ourselves as a Christian group, with an intention to work out our Christian allegiance on the fringe of the churches and within inclusive language and ideas. We feel that God might, and should, be seen as at least as female as male, if indeed gender language is appropriate in the God-context at all. This is the 'given' of our meetings. Within that framework we are happy to welcome anyone to our

St Hilda's has been very good for me because as a deacon I normally can't enjoy my own worship very well. I have to lead it, I have to be responsible for it, and although sometimes I'm responsible for a service here it feels different, and most of the time I can just worship as one of the Community. . . .

What I like best is all the ups and downs, and the fact that it's my only church and a place where one can explore where one is spiritually, be nourished by what one hears. I think what I enjoy most of all is the discussion following the readings as not being a theologian I find that quite exciting and I really love the differences that people pick up in any one passage. I also like to feel that one can worship and at the same time be joyful, angry, questioning and all that I find here. . . .

I came because one of the Sisters came. I had been going to an established church for a long time and I felt that it no longer met my needs. I was tired of having a hierarchy where one person was more powerful than another, and I didn't feel that my needs as a single woman were met at all. What I like about St Hilda's is that there is no leader although I think sometimes it feels a bit directionless. I like very much the variety – the candles, the meditation, the circle dancing. . . .

liturgies regardless of their beliefs, or lack of them. We say that anyone who is there is a member for that evening.

How sectarian are we? We have tended, despite our best intentions, to be rather heavily Anglican, or anyhow ex-Anglican, and one member rebuked us roundly for our enjoyment of 'Anglican gossip'. However inexcusable, this arose partly because so many of our members have been involved in the struggle for women's ordination in the Church of England, a project so consuming while it was going on that it was tempting to talk about it too much. But we have endeavoured to mend our ways.

There have been three important events in the course of St Hilda's history. We published the first edition of this prayer book *Women Included* with SPCK in 1990. Weeks before it emerged, when nothing was publicly known about it except a version of the 'Our Father' by Jim Cotter which addressed God as both father and mother, it was noisily condemned by, *inter alia*, John Gummer, George Austin and the *Daily Telegraph*. Incredibly, questions were asked about it in the House of Commons, and answered in minatory tones by Michael Allison. Rather enjoying the fuss, we carefully harvested all the rude comments and had them tastefully printed on the card which invited the Press and others to the book's launch at the Groucho Club. This event was packed out, and included a magnificent speech by Helena Kennedy QC. As a result of all the publicity *Women Included* sold extremely well.

In November 1992 the General Synod of the Church of England voted to ordain women as priests. Many members of St Hilda's stood outside Church House throughout the day on which voting took place, and, as darkness fell, and candles were lit in a silent vigil, heard with joy the outcome of the day's debate. We opened a bottle of champagne.

A year later five of us – Monica Furlong, Margaret Orr Deas, Brother Thaddaeus, Hannah Ward and Jennifer Wild – protested at General Synod at the Act of Synod which we believed, and believe, to be lacking in theological integrity, and to be insulting to women priests – a distressing sign of a Church of England with cold feet, or, in the bishops' own strange words 'bending over backwards', in this case to accommodate those who refused to acknowledge women priests.

So St Hilda's continued to exercise a public witness. On a private note it continued to be very interested in what a small and radical house church could achieve. After nearly eight years in existence (at the time of writing), the Community has inevitably changed its function some-what since women can now celebrate openly without danger of episco-pal intervention, but there is life there which many inside and outside the Community continue to value.

Last year I was invited to speak to a conference of newly conse-crated bishops and I talked to them about 'green shoots'. It seemed to me that the Church was like an old tree, decrepit with age, possibly fallen. But around its base were innumerable 'green shoots' which continue to derive life from it, and will eventually blossom with Christian flowers.

I pointed out that most of the green shoots were there because of people's sense of being, in one way or another, excluded, unwanted, misunderstood, or not listened to, by the central bodies of the Church. Women were one such group, gay people another. That was not all. Apart from groups like St Hilda's, or LGCM, with a specifically Christian agenda, there were other signs of spiritual growth in the world around us – care for peace, for the environment, for the natural world. There were also new kinds of creative love, attention and self-discipline, being applied to childbirth, child care, death, bereavement, healing, and self-help groups of various kinds, not necessarily identifying with Christianity at all. We seem to be looking at something rather like a spiritual diaspora, with people who have turned at least partially away from the churches writing their own marriage ceremonies (and not only heterosexual couples), and naming ceremonies for children. If church rituals do not feel appropriate to modern people, people are creating their own, such is the need and longing for ritual. Churches too often respond to such information with cries of danger. There may be danger in such enterprise, but it is less than the danger of a society in which all spiritual feeling is dead or taboo. And as St Hilda's long ago discovered, there is nothing like composing one's own liturgy, and writing one's own words, to force one to examine what it is that gives meaning to our transient human lives.

The Community feels as lively as it ever did; my sense is that the commitment of its long-term members to one another has deepened considerably. Whereas we once felt, I think, that we were engaged on a shortish project trying to persuade the Church of England that women must be ordained, now the view has lengthened. We are one of a number of groups who bring to the Church imagination, vitality, a readiness to experiment; unlike the churches we accept and enjoy all-comers. It is not our job to be critical of life-styles, but simply to try to love and appreciate people. It does not seem all that difficult. This is what we think Christianity is all about. Personally, I can think of no membership I would sooner have than being a member of the St Hilda Community.

After the Pentecost celebration I started because although I was very happy in the local church in which I was involved – it is about 95% black and also an exciting congregation to be part of, nevertheless this was another place which affirmed something which was important to me. . . .

Are there things you don't like about St Hilda's?

No, I don't think so. It's just like any other group, ups and downs.

I feel sometimes there's quite a strong feeling of conflict. But I like very much the company of women and feeling that we are all much more equal.

I do think we need to be better at our communication and organization.

A Priest Comes Home *Clare Herbert*

I ATTENDED an ACCM selection conference at the young age of seventeen. My early attendance at such an event was due not to my intensely religious adolescence but to the confusion of the elderly deaconess whose role it was in those days in the Exeter Diocese to help me 'explore my vocation'. She meant, I am sure, to send me to a sixth-form vocations conference, but I ended up at a convent in Ealing putting on as brave a show as I could muster. My only clear memory is of a delightful archdeacon's wife using spare moments to ask me to go down to the pub to buy some cigarettes. It was with glee that I realized that she was a selector, not a candidate, and that I was in with a chance, if her attitude, at least, was anything to go by.

None of this matters much now. What does matter is that I made this show of commitment 25 years ago, in the heady days when we believed the ordination of women to the priesthood was just around the corner. Years later, and by now a young university chaplain and – oh, awful title – 'parish worker', I sat with Jim Cotter at a restaurant table, groaning. How were women going to last the course? How was I going to cope with years of feeling angry with my male colleagues at my lowly position? His reply struck some inner chord, for I remembered it without having any clue how to do what he suggested. 'You must practise your priesthood,' he said, 'That's all.'

It may have looked to the outside world that I did the exact opposite of that suggestion. To cope with my own anger, I retrained as a social worker and enjoyed myself in that career for several years. In fact I realize now that I was always 'practising my priesthood' and the St Hilda Community was a useful place to do it.

To those of us gasping for MOW to grow more rebellious, more theologically and spiritually nourishing, the St Hilda Community became a community of hope. I visited it rarely, since my world was the world of Bristol, but I followed its history in press reports and was ready, when a similar group formed in Bristol, to join in. Once a month in the octagonal chapel of the Polytechnic (now the University of the West of England) a crowd of between 10 and 40 persons attended Chloe's People. CHLOE stood for 'Creative Happenings, Liturgies and Other Events', and was the inspiration of an energetic NSM deacon and social worker, now a canon in Southwark. The emphasis of CHLOE, which consisted of men and women, young and old people and perhaps most strikingly was interdenominational, was the same as that of the St Hilda Community – the creation of liturgies using inclusive language. Numbers waxed and waned during my years in Bristol, but I remember with joy a period when the group met in my own home.

Why did we do it? Why did we meet on Friday evenings, Saturdays and Sunday afternoons to create inclusive-language liturgies? Some of us were already church ministers; why on earth did *we* give it so much

It's quite difficult to keep in contact with people as you just come here on a Sunday and then go away again so the worship is quite valuable but it's difficult to build deeper relationships with people. . . .

As a Methodist lay preacher I have sometimes looked on with bewilderment at the vehemence and anger the issue of women's ordination rouses among Anglicans. Sometimes it has spilled over into the Community as those hurt by institutional religion have turned and hurt one another. . . . God is part of all our messy experience.

Like any community it had its ups and downs – there was something very realistic about the way it dealt with them. But everyone was accepted – there was a lot of new life in the kind of liturgies being produced, both in terms of variations on the traditional themes of the eucharist, but also new ways of treating life as something that was whole and not something set apart. An immense sense of wholeness.

Were there things you didn't like?

There were times when the professional in me (if you will forgive the expression) felt, 'Oh dear, if only things could run more smoothly.'

Do you mean liturgically?

Yes. Yet when things did not go smoothly I liked the way it was accepted, it wasn't, 'Oh help, we got that wrong.'

time? I did it because I gained new energy, and saw a prophetic image of what church might mean. I found the inspiration and support to carry on within the constraints of the institution from this place, this group of people.

The energy came to me from two sources.

First, I found for the first time in my life that liturgy could be formed from the dialogue between my own life-experience and theology. I had experienced services as something handed down to me and the study of liturgy as the study of church history. Of course words and actions in the Eucharist, in readings, sermons and prayers had resonated with my experience before. But never had I been asked to grab the stuff of my own female existence and start there to make a shared act of worship that might sustain, heal and inspire, or, alternatively, bore and distance others. It was as if I had only learned painting by numbers and now someone had thrown away the outlines leaving me the brushes and saying – paint! I remember using the experience of a holiday on Barra, an instance of feeling rejected, and the theme of a year's turning, all as material for liturgy. Strangely, it was not practising the Eucharist which mattered so much. In fact once fears of breaking some enormous taboo were diminished there seemed nothing startling whatever about a woman or a lay person blessing and distributing bread and wine. This *did* matter, of course, in helping us to see that eating and drinking bread and wine, in an act of communion and exploration of the vision of Jesus, cannot be confined to the hierarchies and spaces of the churches. But what mattered far more was the realization of how liturgy well made can form the self, and form community. Liturgy had become pastoral and prophetic for me because areas of my life, as a woman, as a social worker, friend and dreamer were being reclaimed for use.

Second, energy came to me from the possibility created by St Hilda's and other similar groups, of living and talking without fear while speaking of God. Just as the ceiling never fell when a lay person or deacon celebrated the Eucharist, so it never fell when clergy spoke of divorce, or death, or failure, of being lesbian, of struggling to sustain some relationship with parents, of an affair, of hating work, of being lonely. Clergy had nothing to hide – the struggle to love was talked about openly. It was as if a community which could admit of the feminine aspect of the self had no need to hide other aspects.

This freedom to breathe, to say 'what is' with my own voice, in a community of equals, free from the censorship of church hierarchies, has been liberation for me. It is not that I dislike order or have no need for the institution of the Church – far from it – but I find myself reaching mature adulthood as a priest in a Church which is frightened of ambiguity and uncertainty.

One sign of this failure to bear uncertainty as part of the human

There were always fewer men than women in the Community. I wondered how that felt to you as a man?

In a very gentle way it brought home to me the sense of there being a difference, yet not a difference. It came over most in business matters – in most business meetings I have been to there have been a predominance of men yet at St Hilda's business meetings I was sometimes the only man present. Women did things differently.

How?

I think there was always a sense of looking for a consensus. Sometimes, of course, it did come to a case of saying well, who's in favour and who is against. But always there was a desire to get to something that was generally accepted, to carry people with us, and that was quite refreshing. There was something too about the interconnectedness of things – peace, justice, a sense of creation.

condition is that clergy feel pressures put upon them to be different from who they are. Clergy who believe that 'telling it slant' is an essential part of living the gospel are warned that their liberalism has weakened the Church. Women who speak out against appalling acts of insult towards them by fellow and senior clergy and by lay people are made to feel that they ought to be grateful for ordination, to settle down and become less strident. Lesbian and gay clergy are asked to hide their sexual orientation, lest it prove a stumbling-block to faith within their congregations. Internal dissent within the Church is seen as time-wasting navel-gazing, rather than a necessary exploration of what on earth it means for us to follow Christ in the last years of the twentieth century. It is as if everything could become ship-shape by ignoring ourselves and serving the world, without asking the question what sort of people does the world need to have serve it, let alone *want* to have serve it!

St Hilda's, on the other hand, and in my experience, is about talking – talking, arguing even, falling out and in, celebrating, being who one is without risk of censorship. Keeping in touch with who one is and finding the feminine within the self accepted, cherished and challenged creates a sense of 'home-base' for me as a priest. I remember one night, circling around the streets of West London in a car, quarrelling with a friend. We were looking for the Candlemas celebration of St Hilda's, but never made it. The quarrel and a local restaurant won over Candlemas, but the important thing is that it was *there* for me and for many women, on behalf of me and on behalf of many women, like home.

St Hilda's is not the perfect community. At times it is feud-ridden, passive, boring and confused, like any other community. But for a priest like me, wanting to 'come off it', its fragile nature makes it the better container for my humanity. Its existence allows me to come home.

Being a Feminist in the Church *Rachel Carr*

Do you think that was peculiar to this Community or is more to do with attitudes held by women generally?

It is hard to answer because many women like the traditional hierarchical structures – it felt more like the experience one has in a black community of struggling against something and struggling for something. But although there was a sense of struggle, it was accompanied by a sense of celebration, and the feeling that struggling is not just a case of pain and hardship and oppression but that there's something there as well.

There's a real excitement in it?

That's right, that's right.

I first came to St Hilda's as a theological student. We used to come all the way down from Oxford, and it was absolute bliss after the rather austere prayer at college; it was just wonderful to be able to come into more relaxed surroundings. Although I don't come very often it is very good to know that St Hilda's is here. Some kind of vision for something new and different in the Church, which is something to do with being open and flexible. That we are able to allow each individual to contribute in some way – that's very important to me. Because we're such a very widespread, scattered Community it's sometimes hard to know how it does all happen.

M
Y FIRST EXPERIENCE of St Hilda's was in 1988 when the Community still met in Queen Mary College chapel. I was a 23-year-old postgraduate student who was aware of feeling somewhat displaced. A Christian in the English Department was regarded as rather freakish, a feminist Christian worshipping in the traditional college chapel was an almost unheard of species and certainly, for some, a threat. Coming to St Hilda's for the first time was like coming home. I cried during the liturgy. Here, finally, was a place where the distracting anger I experienced in church, which I had just begun to recognize as my reaction to the pervading exclusivity I felt, could be openly and honestly expressed.

It was not, however, until St Hilda's began also to meet in Notting Hill that I began to attend on a regular basis: by then, no longer a student, I was rarely worshipping in church at all. For a period of time St Hilda's became my only spiritual home. After the vote on women's ordination in the Church of England in November 1992 I felt able once again to attend church and in the last three years I have become involved in the spiritual and community life of St Clement's, Notting Dale. Yet, as soon as I 'returned' to the Anglican fold I was forcibly reminded again just how 'radical' explorative and inclusive liturgy appears to most mainstream churches, and how far the Church of England, despite its 1992 vote, still has to go in changing its Victorian attitude to women.

I therefore remain ambivalent about my connection with the Church of England: I want to play a part in changing its attitudes towards women by refusing to let it alienate me; yet how far can one do this without colluding with its oppressive structures? I have found my answer in the St Hilda's Community. Quite simply, worshipping in an institutionalized church would not be possible for me without St Hilda's. I know that for some people the existence of the Community in itself is enough, to know that it is there sending out the message that there are different ways of talking about and experiencing God. For me, this is not enough – I need to be part of it, sustained by it, and, I hope, playing my part in sustaining it, in order to retain any connection with the Anglican Church.

This sounds as if St Hilda's is my spiritual haven, and in one sense it is. The Community, for me, is a space where the feminism that is so central to my 'secular' life can find Christian expression and spiritual exploration. It is a place where it feels entirely natural to feel angry at the Christian tradition's paltry treatment of women. More, it is a place where that anger is channelled creatively, often into laughter. It is a space where I feel set free from many of the ways in which not just the Church but society constricts me. The Community is also a place where I have struggled. Perhaps this is endemic in any spiritual journey.

There was a period when using different ways to speak of God and

I came because I heard Suzanne give a talk. I was struck at once by the level of participation. As a Roman Catholic I cannot participate in any shape or guise in my Church. Even if I have a very sensitive parish priest other than reading and giving out communion I am invisible. So this is a very enabling experience – you do certain things very carefully and you don't have to ask people for permission. Women are very often traumatized. The problem, of course, with every organization that is a non-bureaucratic one, is how do you carry on without an institution. It may be that if the personal charisma goes out then the whole thing falls down. But if it does fall down then that may be a sign of the Spirit. If you keep it going artificially with a very efficient and well-oiled machine of bureaucracy, then you may be answering to a need that is not there. So I don't mind if something collapses, because it had its place, and if it was important it will come back, perhaps in a different guise.

faith came to feel almost stale because it was commonplace. Then I realized how far I still had to go, how using female language as a metaphor for God didn't mean I had ceased to image God in my head as a man with a white beard. I am still surprised to find how deeply ingrained in me is the notion I was brought up with of God the Father. It remains an ongoing effort and a continuing pleasure to explore ways of overcoming this.

I have developed in other ways through my commitment to St Hilda's too. At the beginning it was liberating and exciting when a woman priest celebrated, now it is more important to me that the creation of liturgy and participation in worship is a shared and communal responsibility. I particularly enjoy experiencing liturgy as a dance that can change its steps, and its course of direction, and come into being in the process of its enactment rather than as something requiring a fixed set of responses. I delight in not knowing where I will end up during a St Hilda's liturgy. I have come to rethink and be reinspired about my own participation in contemporary feminism – Christian or otherwise – through relationships with women of my parents' generation whose struggle with a patriarchal religion is so much longer, so different and yet also, in a profound way, so similar to my own. Most importantly, I have learned to experience spirituality and to encounter God at the heart of a dialogue between people from different backgrounds and of different ages, a dialogue that doesn't begin and end with each liturgy but continues in the meal we share and beyond in the friendships I have made.

Circling God *Lillalou Hughes*

CIRCLE DANCING discovered me at the Bristol Cancer Help Centre. It was a revelation. Suddenly I felt properly joined to the earth after years, it seemed, of being caught in a spiritual limbo between heaven and earth. The contact with the floor, or with the ground out of doors, rooted me, it felt, in unity, harmony and healing.

I had always felt awkward dancing, and it was wonderful to feel held in the circle by the joined hands, and to find my balance; above all to realize that if I just kept moving the world did not come to an end if I got the steps wrong. The dancing filled me with energy and relaxed me; a sense of well-being overcame me. As my confidence grew I became deeply aware of the group with whom I danced; a oneness developed as the rhythm took hold of me. And it was fun!

I found a group in London to dance with and gradually discovered more about circle dancing, or sacred dancing as some prefer to call it. It was introduced to Britain at Findhorn in the early 1970s by Bernhard Wosein, a German ballet master. The dances are drawn from the great wealth of ancient dances of Greece, the Slavic countries, the Jewish and Celtic traditions, created for celebrating rituals, meditation and rites of passage. They are ancient ways of expressing emotions and releasing tension.

Some dances are very old, some are new. Circle dance is borrowing from the past and creating for the future, inspiring new compositions and choreography, using folk songs and contemporary tunes, classical and 'pop' music from South Africa, Canada, South America, Latvia, Sweden and Native American tradition.

Circle dance allows the expression of feelings through the many moods of the dances. In our society, which finds the expression of emotion quite difficult, we need to create contexts like this in which we can freely express ourselves. The dance has the potential to take us beyond the limits of our society and its rigid roles. Outside discos, few people in modern western society dance spontaneously; it is usually only the very young who get the chance to do it at all. But like singing it is a vital way of sharing with others, of being 'in tune', or 'in time' with them.

The sacred dance traditions of the world try to remember and repeat the God encounter. By dancing the human-divine encounter, humans are put in touch again with their creative origin. This is the aim and essence of all religious and sacred dance.

When St Hilda's included circle dancing in its liturgies, I was among those who introduced dances there and gradually my confidence as a teacher grew. So often liturgies are wordy, with faith expressed in a very cerebral fashion, as if human beings were minds and nothing else. Using our bodies in worship makes a difference, as if we are bringing our whole being to God. The mood of a liturgy deepens.

There are dances which fit every part of the liturgy – greetings dances, meditative dances, dances based on biblical texts, dances for the

Peace, dances for festivals. Many of them are simple enough for anyone to do; before long people take risks, and learn more complicated dances with more intricate steps and sophisticated rhythms.

That we are embodied, and that our bodies cannot be ignored on our journey with God; that the circle is inclusive, with everyone equally involved; these beliefs go to the heart of what Christian feminists and St Hilda's believe. Our bodies enter a closer experience of ourselves, each other, the world and God.

I feel privileged to share dances at St Hilda's and other liturgy groups, and with groups of women meeting together to make theology, and to share their experiences of their spiritual journey.

Note   Circle Dance tapes with instructions booklets can be obtained. However, it is better to attend a workshop before attempting to teach dances, and many circle dance groups advertise in local libraries. A local teacher may be willing to arrange a teaching afternoon or evening for you.

Tapes are available from Dancing Circles, Wesley Cottage, New Road, East Huntspill, Highbridge, Somerset TA9 3PT. Other information about circle dancing may be obtained via the Network journal 'Grapevine', c/o 14 Manor House Road, Jesmond, Newcastle-upon-Tyne NE2 2LU (enclose s.a.e.).

Part Two

How It Works *Monica Furlong*

A T ST HILDA's all our services take place in a circle, either round the table upon which we eat our meal, or in chairs in an adjoining room preparatory to going to the table to have supper together. One or two people will have prepared the liturgy, and chosen readers or any material needed, such as a tape for dancing. Others will have telephoned round to check on the food for the evening, to see who feels like bringing a first course, bread, home-made or otherwise, salads, sweets and wine. The food never turns out to be scrappy or unsatisfying – preparing it carefully is part of our preparation for the liturgy. This feels a very female way of 'being religious', as if it is impossible for women to separate the sense of hospitality from worship, or to believe in a Eucharist that is divorced from a normal meal. It makes us wonder whether church practices might have been very different if women had been included in the planning from the beginning.

The first quarter of an hour is devoted to 'catching up' on one another. People arrive tired from travelling or from the day's work, and we sit quietly and chat. Newcomers are welcomed and introduced as 'old hands' arrive. We unpack the food, see what needs to go into the oven, and gradually move into a deeper quietness together.

The leader for the evening will begin by describing the form the service will take and, if there are a lot of people present, asking them to introduce themselves individually. St Hilda's has always had a constant stream of visitors, as well as people wanting to join themselves to us more permanently, and we try to make both feel they have a place.

We strive for informality and participation in our liturgies – if people feel stupid, overawed, shy, or frightened of doing the wrong thing then we have failed. Comments and ad lib jokes during a service seem to come naturally to us – it does not seem to spoil the atmosphere; on the contrary – and newcomers are invited to join in fully with readings, intercessions and ritual. Liturgy tends to be spoken either in unison (this only really works with fairly short sentences, otherwise it gets rather lugubrious), or going round and round the circle with one person at a time speaking a paragraph or a sentence. The intention is to make everyone feel included and equally valued.

There are opening prayers, some form of asking for forgiveness, intercession, readings, the peace, a sharing of bread and wine and a blessing at all our services. In others, with a greater degree of formality, depending on the occasion and the numbers, there may be hymns, dancing, an offertory. The peace seems extraordinarily warm after the cool handshakes and pecks on the cheek of exchanges of the peace in other places.

Each service has its own quality. Partly because a number of us have been worshipping together for years we tend to be sensitive to each other's moods – to know who is depressed, anxious, in crisis, or feeling they need to celebrate. Making a cross on each other's foreheads, reminding our neighbour to forgive others and to forgive themselves, is a very real recognition of our inner conflicts. Partly through the intercessions in which we each light a candle and mention names, we also become aware of a network of other people not personally known to us – parents, children, grandchildren, friends, workmates, pupils – who unbeknown to them are part of St Hilda's life. We share in birth, death, marriage, work problems, illness, success and failure. Usually too we bring into the intercession period the darkness and joy of the world in which we live. We also recognize in one another the right to silence – *not* to feel that we have to share our innermost thoughts unless it feels like the right time and place. This sort of respect and reticence seems a good way to be together. By the time we are ready to pass round the bread and the wine we have already 'communicated' with one another in some depth.

Opening Prayers

F<small>ROM THE</small> fragmented world of our everyday lives
We gather together in search of wholeness.
By many cares and preoccupations
by diverse and separate aims
are we separated from one another
and divided within ourselves.
Yet we know that no branch is utterly severed
From the Tree of life that sustains us all.

W<small>E HAVE</small> come together in this quiet space
to reflect upon our lives in the light of the Christian mystery.
To pray for ourselves and others.
To deepen the sense of affection and understanding we have for each
other, women for women, men for men, and women and men for one another.

B<small>E</small> silent.
Be still.
Alone. Empty
before your God.
Say nothing.
Ask nothing.
Be silent.
Be still.
Let your God
look upon you.
That is all.
She knows.
She understands.
She loves you with
an enormous love.
She only wants to
look upon you
with her love.
Quiet.
Still.
Be.

Let your God –
Love you.

1   O G<small>OD</small>, I seek you while you may be found;
2   I call upon you while you are near.
3   O God, you are my Redeemer,
    abundant in forgiveness and love.
4   Your thoughts are not our thoughts,
    neither are your ways our ways.
5   As the rain and the snow come down from the skies
    and return not again but water the earth,
6   bringing forth life and giving growth,
    seed for the sowing and bread for the eating;
7   so the Word that goes forth from your mouth
    will not return to you empty,
8   but it will accomplish that which you purpose
    and succeed in the task that you give it.

Be in love with life

wrestle with the chaos and the pain

with yourself and with others

spirit echoing Spirit

trusting in the victory of the vulnerable;

glimpsing the peace,

the wholeness,

the spaciousness,

the justice,

**and the joy
that comes from following the Pioneer**

made perfect in suffering;

**striving and yearning and crying out
from the very depths and heights
of the world's anguish and the world's bliss,**

and so becoming friends and partners of God
in the divine creating.

Loving God,
together we seek the way,
helping, watching, learning, leading,
each step forging new links,
each dialogue opening further
the channels of peace and understanding.
We stand poised on the brink of greatness,
drawn by the Spirit into new realms of hope and trust.
The barriers of past centuries are slowly crumbling.
We pray that the skeletons of division and discord
will be laid to rest,
and that the people of God will be fully mobilized.
For these and all your mercies,
we thank and praise you O God.

In the beginning,
in the very beginning,
God gave birth to,
God delivered,
God created
the heavens and the earth.
Yes, out of the womb
of fertile divinity
emerged our mother,
the earth.

Mother earth, sister sea, giving
birth, energy,
reaching out, touching me
lovingly.

The living God,
The living, moving Spirit of God
has called us together –
in witness, in celebration, in struggle.

Reach out toward each other
(We all stand and hold hands)
Our God reaches out toward us.

Let us worship God.
(Drop hands)

GOD OUR father and our mother,
you have made us for yourself,
our hearts are restless
till they find their rest in you.
Teach us to offer ourselves to your service,
that here we may have your peace,
and in the world to come may see you face to face:
through Jesus Christ, our Friend and Brother.

1   WE COME together
in thankfulness and joy
for a place in which to pray
For others with whom to pray

2   For a God to whom to pray.
May our eyes be opened wide
Our ears be sharp to listen

3   Our tongues speak the truth
Our minds feed upon the truth

4   Our hearts be softened by the truth.

WE ARE the meeting place of heaven and earth, soul and body, breath and blood,
and we celebrate you with every part of our being.
You are Eternal, while we remain within the passage of time, measuring our span in numbers.
All, Jesus our Brother, whose incarnation was the meeting place of time and eternity,
teach us to take joy in the earth and the heavens.
Let us rejoice in our mortality and its loves,
and sing aloud when our soul reaches out for the stars,
for by both we prove we are God's children.

O GOD who gives all that is good,
may your blessing be upon our food,
your grace and laughter shine upon our fellowship,
your kindness be upon our tongues,
your peace reside within us,
and your love reign in our hearts. Amen.

GLORIOUS GOD, ever-present in our lives,
give us courage to face our difficulties;
strengthen and inspire us when we are overcome by doubt and anguish;
hold us in love and compassion when we knowingly do what is wrong;
forgive us and help us to forgive ourselves,
and help us to acknowledge your presence, now and always.

DEAR GOD

Many of us struggle with how we may think and speak of you
in a way that makes sense, in our lives and in our world.
As we struggle, we continue to address you . . . the ground of our being . . .
the Spirit within . . .

For we believe that somehow you give meaning in our lives –
we believe that if you are about anything
then somehow you are also everything.

And so you are in our unknowing and our searching
and in our groping after truth.
You are in our aloneness and our vulnerability;
in our anger, envy and inner chaos,
and in our struggle to be free.
You are part of our impotence
and you are in our empowering.
You are in the emptiness
and also in the filling up.
You are at the roots of despair and brokenness
and also the way that leads to connection.

WE HAVE come together this evening
seeking for space to be ourselves . . .
And looking for sustenance from being with others . . .
Hoping to find strength as we join in our common search
for that which gives meaning and purpose to our lives.
As we share something of ourselves
may we grow closer to the Spirit which brings us here.

The Gloria

We adore the glory and the truth that is God.
Everything within us utters praise.
Our being is formed for this purpose and no other.
All our loves and works find meaning in you.

Jesus, who shows us what God is like,
forgive us our failure to understand
but keep us in your dazzling presence.

For there we learn the nature of holiness
and partake with you in the secret of the godhead.

Glory be to you,   Ground of all Being,
Source of all Strength,
Giver of all Power.
Amen.

1   Glory in all my seeing
Glory in all my being
2   Glory in all my speaking
Glory in all my seeking
3   Glory in all my hearing
Glory in every appearing
4   Glory in all my feeling
Glory in God's revealing
5   Glory of the mighty Three
Glory entwining round me
6   Glory in the opening day
Glory in the rocky way
7   Glory in the morning light
Glory in the darkest night
8   Glory there for beholding
Glory ever me enfolding.

9   Glory of God
Hand above
10 Glory of Christ
Heart of love
11 Glory of Spirit
Covering dove.

Glory to God, glory to God,
glory to our maker.
Glory to God, glory to God,
glory to our maker.
To God be glory forever.
To God be glory forever.
Alleluia. Amen.
Alleluia. Amen.
Alleluia. Amen.
Alleluia. Amen.

Glory to Christ, glory to Christ,
glory to our brother.
Glory to Christ, glory to Christ,
glory to our brother.
To Christ be glory forever.
To Christ be glory forever.
Alleluia. Amen.
Alleluia. Amen.
Alleluia. Amen.
Alleluia. Amen.

Glory to God, glory to God,
glory to the Spirit.
Glory to God, glory to God,
glory to the Spirit
Give us your freedom forever.
Give us your freedom forever.
Alleluia. Amen.
Alleluia. Amen.
Alleluia. Amen.
Alleluia. Amen.

Collects

Jesus, who was lost and found in the garden,
never to be lost again
Stand by us in the darkness of our crucifixions,
as the women stood by you.
Die and rise with us in the suffering of the world.
Be reborn with us
as love and hope and faith and endurance
outlast cruelty and death. Amen.

O God our deliverer,
you cast down the mighty,
and lift up those of no account;
as Elisabeth and Mary embraced
with songs of liberation,
so may we also be pregnant with your Spirit,
and affirm one another in hope for the world,
through Jesus Christ. Amen.

O God, the power of the powerless,
you have chosen as your witnesses
those whose voice is not heard.
Grant that, as women first announced
the Resurrection
though they were not believed,
we too may have courage
to persist in proclaiming your word,
In the power of Jesus Christ. Amen.

God of the outsider
who in your servant Ruth
established the line of our salvation;
give us her love and courage
with all the women who wait
like strangers in your church,
to travel a new path;
put our faith in the faith of a woman,
and boldly claim your promise,
through Jesus Christ. Amen.

GOD WHOSE body is all creation,
may we come to know you in all the earth
and feel you in our blood;
so will no part of us, or the world,
be lost to your transforming grace.
Amen.

FLAME-DANCING Spirit, come
Sweep us off our feet and
Dance us through our days.
Surprise us with your rhythms;
Dare us to try new steps, explore
New patterns and new partnerships;
Release us from old routines
To swing in abandoned joy and
Fearful adventure. And
In the intervals,
Rest us
In your still centre. Amen.

SPIRIT OF Truth
whom the world can never grasp,
touch our hearts
with the shock of your coming;
fill us with desire
for your disturbing peace;
and fire us with longing
to speak your uncontainable word,
through Jesus Christ. Amen.

CHRIST OUR healer,
beloved and remembered by women,
Speak to the grief which makes us forget,
and to the terror that makes us cling,
and give us back our name;
that we may greet you clearly
and proclaim your risen life. Amen.

GOD OUR deliverer
whose approaching birth still shakes
the foundations of our world,
may we so wait for your coming
with eagerness and hope
that we embrace without terror
the labour pangs of the new age,
through Jesus Christ. Amen.

THANKS BE to God that we have risen this day
– To the rising of this life itself.

Be the purpose of God between us and each purpose.
The hand of God between us and each hand.
The pain of Christ between us and each pain.
The love of Christ between us and each love.

CHRIST, OUR only true light,
before whose bright cloud
your friends fell to the ground;
we bow before your cross
that we may remember in our bodies
the dead who fell like shadows;
and that we may refuse to be prostrated
before the false brightness
of any other light,
looking to your power alone
for hope of resurrection from the dead.
Amen.

O GRACIOUS God
You bring us together from many different places,
You endow us with varied gifts and responsibilities,
You challenge us to respond to your call.
Guide our halting, impatient steps,
Sustain us and help us sustain each other,
that, through our labours
We may help bring into the world
your sweet justice,
through Jesus our Redeemer. Amen.

LET THY Resurrection light radiate all our worship
by the power of the Holy Spirit.
Help us to know ourselves
as women and men who have been made new.
By that same power inspire us to walk
even as he walked;
that going on our way in faith and gladness
we may come at last to those things which eye hath not seen
nor ear heard
but which thou hast prepared for all them that truly love thee
from the beginning of the world. Amen.

GOD OUR mother,
you hold our life within you;
nourish us at your breast,
and teach us to walk alone.
Help us so to receive your tenderness
and respond to your challenge
that others may draw life from us,
in your name. Amen.

SPIRIT OF integrity,
you drive us out into the desert
to search out your truth.
Give us clarity to know what is right,
and courage to reject what is expedient;
that we may abandon the false innocence
of failing to choose at all;
but may follow the purposes of Jesus Christ.
Amen.

O CHRIST THE Risen Word,
raise us with you in this glorious Easter season.
Nurture the resurrection life in us.
Send your Spirit where the new season dances
and brings us into the full promise of Spring.
Amen.

Confessions of Faith

WE BELIEVE in the presence of God in the world.

She is our mother, source of deep wisdom, who:
> holds and protects us,
> nourishes our bodies,
> comforts our pain,
> hears and accepts our times of failure and success.

She is our lover and is allowed to touch our pain:
> healing and recreating,
> seeking out what is hidden,
> revealing deep, precious mysteries.

She is our friend who stands alongside us:
> working co-operatively for the common good,
> sharing our concerns,
> fiercely criticizing our lack of integrity.

We believe in the presence of God in our world.
We meet her as people met her in Jesus, in countless relationships
which are at once human and divine:
> in simple encounters with men, women and children,
> in office and schoolroom, home and supermarket,
> in the community of her people.

We believe in the presence of God in our world,
whose truth is denied, in anguish, like that of Jesus on the cross,
whenever:
> food is withheld,
> the earth is poisoned, abused or destroyed,
> people are oppressed, denied dignity and responsibility,
> tortured or killed.

Together we affirm the truth and goodness of God, our mother, lover
and friend and commit ourselves to her in following the way of our brother Jesus.

Leader   WE BELIEVE in God
All   Who created women and men in God's own image;
who created the world and gave both sexes the care of the earth.

Leader   We believe in Jesus
All   Child of God, chosen by God, born of the woman Mary;
who listened to women and stayed in their homes,
who looked for the kingdom with them,
who was followed and supported by women disciples.

Leader   We believe in Jesus
All   Who discussed theology with a woman at a well,
who received anointing from a woman at Simon's house,
and who rebuked the men guests who scorned her.

Leader   We believe in Jesus
All   Who healed a woman on the Sabbath,
who spoke of God as a woman seeking a lost coin –
as a woman who swept, seeking the lost.

Leader   We believe in Jesus
All   Who thought of pregnancy and birth with reverence.

Leader   We believe in Jesus
All   Who appeared first to Mary Magdalene,
and sent her with the message – 'Go and tell'.

Leader   We believe in the wholeness of God
All   In whom there is neither Jew nor Greek, slave nor free,
male nor female, for all are one in God.

Leader   We believe in the Holy Spirit
All   As she moves over the waters of creation, and over the earth;
the woman spirit of God, who created us and gave us birth
and covers us with her wings.

THE DRAMA OF CREATION

Leader	IN THE beginning, God made the world:
Women	Made it and mothered it,
Men	Shaped it and fathered it;
Women	Filled it with seed and with signs of fertility,
Men	Filled it with love and its folk with ability.
Leader	All that is green, blue, deep and growing,
All	God's is the hand that created you.
Leader	All that crawls, flies, swims, walks or is motionless,
All	God's is the hand that created you.
Leader	All that speaks, sings, cries, laughs or keeps silence,
All	God's is the hand that created you.
Leader	All that suffers, lacks, limps or longs for an end,
All	God's is the hand that created you.
Leader	The world belongs to the Lord,
All	The earth and its people are his.

THE DRAMA OF THE INCARNATION

Leader	WHEN THE time was right, God sent the Son.
Women	Sent him and suckled him,
Men	Reared him and risked him;
Women	Filled him with laughter and tears and compassion,
Men	Filled him with anger and love and devotion.
Leader	Unwelcomed child, refugee and runaway,
All	Christ is God's own son.
Leader	Skilled tradesman and redundant carpenter,
All	Christ is God's own son.
Leader	Feeder and teacher, healer and antagonist,
All	Christ is God's own son.
Leader	Lover of the unlovable, toucher of the untouchable, forgiver of the unforgivable,
All	Christ is God's own son.
Leader	Loved by women, feared by men; befriended by the weak, despised by the strong; deserted by his listeners, denied by his friends; bone of our bone, flesh of our flesh, writing heaven's pardon over earth's mistakes.
All	Christ is God's own son.
Leader	The Word became flesh,
All	He lived among us, he was one of us.

WE BELIEVE in God
>   Maker, Redeemer and Sustainer of Life
>   without beginning or end.
>   whose life-giving love was let loose on the first Easter Sunday
>   and whose life-giving love we share and proclaim here today.

We believe in God
>   who gave up the divine life and submitted to the darkness
>   and terror of the grave
>   and who enters with us into every darkness and terror we
>   shall ever face.

We believe in God
>   who raised Christ from the death of the grave to glorious
>   new life
>   and who raises our lives from sin and despair to newness
>   and hope again.

We believe in God
>   who met the grief-stricken Mary in the garden and called her
>   into hope by the uttering of her name.
>   and who meets us in our grief and gives us courage to hope
>   again by tenderly calling our name.

We believe in God
>   who sent Mary out from the garden to be the witness and
>   apostle of the resurrection
>   and who commissions us, like Mary, to be bearers of hope
>   and good news in our world.

We believe in God
>   Maker, Redeemer and Sustainer of Life.
>   without beginning or end,
>   whose life-giving love was let loose on the first Easter Sunday
>   and whose life-giving love we share and proclaim today
>   to all women and men, wherever and whoever they are,
>   loved, blessed and called by God,
>   without beginning or end.

Discussion

There are usually two and, sometimes, three readings at St Hilda's services, often taken from the lectionary of the Alternative Service Book. Sometimes one or two are taken from other sources, poetry, news stories, or other material. When they are finished there is a silence and then anyone present may comment. At times it may be a good idea to suggest that no one speaks more than once, and to restrict the discussion to a certain length of time, say ten minutes. If there is a large number of people it may be better to divide into small groups.

Intercessions

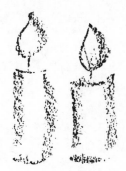

At every St Hilda's service there is a bowl of sand with one large candle burning in the middle of it, and a basket with small candles standing beside it. At the time of the intercessions we sit in silence for five to ten minutes. When they wish, worshippers get up, light a small candle from the bigger one, and place it beside it in the sand, saying 'I light this candle for . . .' naming their purpose e.g. the homeless, the hungry, X who is ill, Y who is dying, A and B who are going through a bad time in their marriage. Or they may say 'I light this candle in gratitude for . . .' e.g. an illness they have recovered from, some good event in their lives, etc. Or they may prefer to light the candle in silence.

Sometimes alternatively a lighted candle is passed from one person to another, with each naming their subject of intercession when the candle is handed to them, or simply holding the candle for a moment before passing it on.

I LIGHT the candle,
the light shines out,
the candle is transformed,
the spirit gives of herself,
we all receive.

SISTERS AND brothers of the Community of St Hilda,
Apart and part of the whole,
In isolation and in communion,
Near and far,
Together we pray:

Heal us, Creator God, that we may become whole;
Inspire us, Spirit of God, and instil in us new wisdom;
Lead us, brother Jesus, to love and serve each other;
Defeating the fears which lead to discrimination;
Affirming all women and men as celebrants in the eucharist of life.

GOD OF justice and peace, you stand with those who are poor,
You ask us to be the voice of the voiceless.
We call upon you for those who have suffered the injustice
of war and greed, from the depths of our being we cry to you:

Creator God, you know what we need, without our words.
Hear our prayer and hear also our silence. Grant us those
things we cannot or dare not voice. We make these prayers
through our brother Jesus. Amen.

1 INTO YOUR hands, Lord,
2 This solitude,
3 Into your hands, Lord,
4 This emptiness.
5 Into your hands, Lord
6 This loneliness.
7 Into your hands –
8 This all.
9 Into your hands, O Lord,
10 This grief.
11 Into your hands,
12 This sleeping fear.
All Into your hands, O Lord –
   What is left,
   What is left
   Of me.

All FROM THE flowing of the tide
   to its ebbing
   From the waxing of life
   to its waning

1 Of your Peace provide us
2 Of your Light lead us
3 Of your Goodness give us
4 Of your Grace grant us
5 Of your Power protect us
6 Of your Love lift us

All And in your arms accept us
   From the ebbing of the tide
   to its flowing
   From the waning of life
   to its waxing.

FORGIVING and understanding God
Help us to use our energy wisely

   to appreciate what we so often take for granted
   to love ourselves, imperfect as we are
   to love and accept others as they are
   to love you and accept and trust your love for us – always.

Loving and all-knowing God
Help us to remember you
when we are angry
when we are disappointed
when we are lonely
when we are unhappy
when we are joyful

**And, having remembered you,
enable us to acknowledge and feel your
presence in us.**

1 God, free us from our anxiety, from our obsession with details,
from our greed for possessions, from our fear of loss.
2 Free us from our laziness and from our overworking,
from our attempts to fill our loneliness with busyness.
3 Release us from our clumsiness, our awkwardness,
our selfishness with others, so that rejoicing wholeheartedly in
their happiness, and entering sensitively into their suffering
we may become learned in the school of love.
4 Make us brave.
5 Make us truthful.
6 Make us people who have the faith to change the world.

All **Give us love.**

Are you there? In:
the slaughter of war
the terror of disasters
the anguish of death
the torment of pain
the pain of bereavement
the horror of crimes.

We long to be assured and comforted when darkness overwhelms us.
Loving God, hear our cries and grant us peace. Amen.

Litany

FOR THE darkness of waiting
of not knowing what is to come
of staying ready and quiet and attentive,
we praise you O God.

**For the darkness and the light
are both alike to you**

For the darkness of staying silent
for the terror of having nothing to say
and for the greater terror
of needing to say nothing,
we praise you O God.

**For the darkness and the light
are both alike to you**

For the darkness of loving
in which it is safe to surrender
to let go of our self-protection
and to stop holding back our desire,
we praise you, O God.

**For the darkness and the light
are both alike to you**

For the darkness of choosing
when you give us the moment
to speak, and act, and change,
and we cannot know what we have set
in motion,
but we still have to take the risk,
we praise you O God.

**For the darkness and the light
are both alike to you**

For the darkness of hoping
in a world which longs for you,
for the wrestling and the labouring of
all creation
for wholeness and justice and
freedom,
we praise you O God.

**For the darkness and the light
are both alike to you**

BLESSING THE BREAD
(a litany for four voices)

1   IN THE beginning was God
2   In the beginning, the source of
    all that is.
3   In the beginning, God yearning
4   God, moaning
1   God, labouring
2   God, giving birth
3   God, rejoicing
4   And God loved what she
    had made
1   And God said, 'It is good'.

2   Then God, knowing that all
    that is good is shared
3   Held the earth tenderly in
    her arms.
4   God yearned for relationship.
1   God longed to share the
    good earth.
2   And humanity was born in the
    yearning of God.
3   We were born to share the earth.

4   In the earth was the seed
1   In the earth was the grain
2   In the grain was the harvest
3   In the harvest was the bread
4   In the bread was the power.

1   And God said, All shall eat
    of the earth
2   All shall eat of the seed.
3   All shall eat of the grain
4   All shall eat of the harvest.
1   All shall eat of the bread.
2   All shall eat of the power.
3   God said, You are my people
4   My friends,
1   My lovers,
2   My sisters,
3   And brothers,
4   All of you shall eat
1   Of the bread
2   And the power
3   All shall eat

4   Then God, gathering up her
    courage in love, said,

1   Let there be bread!
2   And God's sisters, her friends
    and lovers, knelt on the earth
3   planted the seeds
4   prayed for the rain
1   sang for the grain
2   made the harvest
3   cracked the wheat
4   pounded the corn
1   kneaded the dough
2   kindled the fire
3   filled the air with the smell
    of fresh bread
4   And there was bread!
1   And it was good!

2   We, the sisters of God, say today
3   All shall eat of the bread,

4 And the power,
1 We say today,
2 All shall have power
3 And bread,
4 Today we say
1 Let there be bread.
2 And let there be power!
3 Let us eat of the bread and
    the power!
4 And all will be filled
1 For the bread is rising!

2 By the power of God
3 Women are blessed,
4 By the women of God
1 The bread is blessed
2 By the bread of God
3 the power is blessed
4 By the power of bread
1 the power of women
2 the power of God
3 The people are blessed.

All The earth is blessed
     And the bread is rising.

Forms of Confession

We need your forgiveness, merciful God,
For not allowing our complacency to be shattered,
For taking refuge too often in the familiar and the certain;
For not believing in the victory of vulnerability,
For not daring to accept your gifts nor claim your promises.
Grant us true repentance.
Set us free to hear your word to us.
Set us free to serve you.

I deny God's gifts in me
and I deny God's gifts in others.
I ask forgiveness.

God forgives you. Forgive yourself. Be at peace.

O God, we bring you our failure,
our hunger, our disappointment, our despair,
our greed, our aloofness, our loneliness.
When we cling to others in desperation
Or turn from them in fear
Strengthen us in love.
Teach us, women and men
To use our power with care.

We turn to you, O God,
We renounce evil,
We claim your love,
We choose to be made whole.

All God, you know us as we are;
you know our selfishness,
our anger and bitterness,
our fear and apathy,
our hardness of heart,
our deliberate blindness,
our need to begin again.

Leader In your mercy and love,

All Forgive us, change and renew us.

WE CONFESS our failure to live our lives to the full
or to help others to do this,
our inability to recognize you in others
or in the world about us,
our impatience with ourselves and others when we do not live up to
your image within us.

KEEPER AND Companion of us all, forgive us.

You call us, like Eve, to co-create new worlds;
But we turn away and backslide into the comfortable or the certain.

You call us, like Miriam, to dance for freedom;
But we turn away and glory in how far we have come, forgetting how
far we have to go.

You call us, like Deborah, to judge our world, to make decisions and
offer counsel;
But we turn away and apologise for our anger and compromise our
positions.

You call us, like Naomi and Ruth, to love one another;
But we turn away and compete, taking vengeance on those most
like ourselves.

You call us, like Mary, to be faithful bearers of your word;
But we turn away and strive to become perfectionists.

You call us, like Thecla and Phoebe, to begin a new church;
But we turn away and accept a place in the system, rationalizing
things the way they are.

Merciful Healer, we do not claim our gifts. We do not face up to
your call. We do not appreciate your partnership in creating a new
community and a new world. Today we repent. We turn from our old
ways and commit ourselves to new partnerships for holding on and to
new visions for a different heaven and earth.

Leader I WILL POUR clean water upon you,
says God, our mother,
and you shall be clean
from all your uncleanness;
from all your idols I will cleanse you. (Ez. 36:25)

All Wash away my guilt, O God,
and cleanse me from my sin. (Ps. 51:2)

Leader Let us call to mind a particular failing
which we would like to have washed away.

1 GOD OF love and forgiveness
Save us by your tenderness
2 From each deed of evilness
3 From each act of sinfulness
4 From each thought of carelessness
5 From each idea of wickedness
6 From each word of hurtfulness
7 From each speech of harmfulness

All Save us by your tenderness
God of love and forgiveness.

Absolution

The person presiding at the service turns to the person on her/his left and makes the sign of the cross on their forehead, saying 'God forgives you. Forgive others. Forgive yourself' or one of the similar forms given here. That person in turn passes the absolution to the person on her/his left. Sometimes oil is used to make the sign of the cross, and sometimes, alternatively to the above, we wash and dry the hands of the person sitting next to us.

GOD forgives you
Forgive others
Forgive yourself

BE healed, be whole.

WOMAN/Man, your sins are forgiven,
Go in peace.

The Peace

At the time of the Peace we get up from the circle and walk around touching or embracing one another. The Peace is usually the time we place money in the Offertory bowl.

Peace I leave with you,
My own peace I give to you.

May Christ's peace invade, flood and shake the
foundations of our hearts and lives, in this
Community, in our daily lives, in our witness
to the world; let peace BREAK OUT!

Brother/Sister, be at peace.

Peace and love are always alive in us, but we are
not always alive to peace and love.

We meet together to share this meal,
may it express our love for one another
our commitment to each other
and point us beyond ourselves
to the needs of the world.

The peace of God be with you all.

And also with you.

PEACE is flowing like a river, flowing out through you and me
Spreading out into the desert, setting all the captives free.

Love is flowing like a river. . . .

Joy is flowing like a river. . . .

Hope is flowing like a river. . . .

AND OUR approach was in peace,
And we were established in the Spirit of unity.

GOD MAKES peace within us.
Let us claim it.
God makes peace between us.
Let us share it.

The Offertory

WE HOLD UP our smallness to your greatness,
our fear to your love.
Our tiny act of giving to your great generosity
Ourselves to you.

GOD BE with you
And with your spirit.
We turn our faces to God
we offer our hearts.

WE COME with offerings – of our time,
our money, our strength,
our pleasure in one another's company.
All these we bring to God in dedication,
and for use in the glory of the realm of God.

As each person brings the offerings of bread, wine, water and a candle, all say:

The bread THE BREAD we bring, is it not a sharing of the
Body of Christ?

The wine The cup of blessing which we bring, is it not a sharing
of the Blood of Christ?

The water God our Mother, you wash us and cleanse us and
come among us as One who serves.

The candle In the beginning, when it was very dark, God said,
Let there be light.

Prayer of Jesus

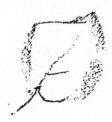

God, who cares for us,
The wonder of whose presence fills us with awe.
Let kindness, justice and love shine in our world.
Let your secrets be known here as they are in heaven.
Give us the food and the hope we need for today.
Forgive us our wrongdoing
as we forgive the wrongs done to us.
Protect us from pride and from despair
and from the fear and hate which can swallow us up.
In you is truth, meaning, glory and power,
while worlds come and go. Amen.

Beloved,
our Father and Mother,
in whom is heaven.
Hallowed be your name,
followed by your royal way,
done be your will and rule,
throughout the whole creation.
With the bread we need for today,
feed us,
In the hurts we absorb from one another,
forgive us.
In times of temptation and test,
strengthen us.
From trials too great to endure,
spare us.
From the grip of all that is evil,
free us.
For you reign in the glory
of the power that is love,
now and forever. Amen.

God, lover of us all, most holy one,
help us to respond to you,
to create what you want for us here on earth.
Give us today enough for our needs;
forgive our weak and deliberate offences,
just as we must forgive others when they hurt us.
Help us to resist evil and to do what is good;
for we are yours,
endowed with your power to make us whole.
Amen.

Seasonal Prayers

ADVENT

(At the beginning of Advent)

I OPEN this season of Advent by lighting the first of the Advent candles.
May it be for us a time of waiting, in peace and hope, for the joy that our faith
promises us in the new life of Jesus.

(At the lighting of the Advent candles)

LET US be a light to the world as this candle is a light to us.
Let us strive for love, justice, truth and joy.
Let us care for others as for ourselves
And for ourselves as for others.

CHRISTMAS

WE STAND at the turning of the year, the time of death and birth, of
darkness and light, of sadness and joy, and we remember the baby born in a
stable who pours glory upon our lives. As we give presents to one another
we recognize the love present in our world, a love that redeems the cruelty,
pain and fear.

MAY THE SPIRIT of Jesus be born in us this Christmas and be cradled in our
hearts. May it bring us life – the life of laughter and generosity and
kindness and joy. May it quicken our imaginations. May its presence
drive away fear and anxiety and greed and shame. May it heal us and others.
May it grow in us into wisdom and love.

EPIPHANY

TODAY WE share bread and wine together in memory of the birth of a baby, of the star and the journey, of the courage of those who seek to give themselves. May the light of God shine upon us in our struggles and hopes, our griefs and disappointments. May the journey bring us joy. May its ending bring us our heart's desire.

WE SEEK to be transformed, and the bread and the wine are the symbols of that transformation, of the secret of God which burns in our hearts. Show us how to recognize God, and recognizing, to adore. Make us faithful to the truth of which the star reminds us. Let not money or success or greed or desire lead us astray.

MAY THE STAR which shone upon kings and wise men shine upon us till we are dazzled by its beauty and ready to commit the folly of a journey, there to surrender our tiny possessions and our timid beliefs. Reveal to us, as we can bear it, the mystery and the joy.

LENT

We need time, space, simplicity in our lives – enough bareness to discern the outline of who we are and how we should live. Let us use Lent as a time of peace and reflection, in which we withdraw from getting and spending and desiring, and remember the love which upholds us.

Lent is a time for clarity, as when the bare boughs of winter show us the shape of the tree in austere beauty. Let us clear away the clutter of our lives in order to see the underlying pattern.

EASTER

We worship the God who entered the extreme of human suffering, and who revealed to us the pattern – that joy and life are the other side of pain and death. We hold up the unspeakable suffering we see around us in the world to the tragic figure on the cross, and it is returned to us in the energy, hope and glory of the resurrection. God who imitated us, work out the divine pattern in each of us, that our lives may be transformed.

PENTECOST

The holiness of the dove,
the cleansing fire,
the strong wind,
work upon our souls
to make us
the people we must be,
the people of your kingdom
able to speak in one another's tongue.

HARVEST

Long live the child.
Long live the mother and father.
Long live the people.

Long live this wounded planet.
Long live the good milk of the air.
Long live the spawning river and the mothering oceans.
Long live the juice of the grass
    and all the determined greenery of the globe.
Long live the surviving animals.
Long live the earth, deeper than all our thinking.

We have done enough killing.

Long live the man
Long live the woman
Who use both courage and compassion.
Long live their children.

'The Final Chant' by Adrian Mitchell

PRAYER FOR JUSTICE AND PEACE

O GOD, gentle and generous, creator of the infinitely huge and the
infinitely little, we ask you to look lovingly on your heart-broken world.
May wholeness and peace be manifest, may your kingdom come,
and may the spirit of agape prevail. Amen.

PRAYER OF THANKSGIVING

For moments of laughter,
for times of joyful sharing,
for the happiness we feel for family and friends,
for moments of peace within us
we give thanks.
Help us, loving God, to remember them when our lives are difficult and
    stressful.
Help us at all times to remember that you are always with us and to give thanks
    for that.

Agape

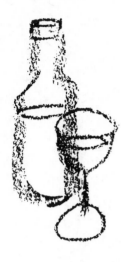

BE GENTLE when you touch bread;
let it not lie uncared for, unwanted.
So often bread is taken for granted.
There is such beauty in bread –
beauty of sun and soil,
beauty of patient toil.
Wind and rain have caressed it.
Christ often blessed it.
So let us be gentle in touching bread.

Keep sober when you drink wine.
Let it not be wasted or taken in vain,
nor like water washed down a drain.
There is the deepest art in the creation of wine.
Choice of the right soil;
skill in dressing the vine
judgement of the right time of harvest;
craft of transforming the grapes into wine.
Christ saw it poured out and spilt as his blood.
Let wine not be misunderstood.

I am quiet now before God
As a child lies quietly in its mother's arms
As a child that lies quiet is my soul. (Ps. 131:2)

AS WOMEN bake bread and share it with their families,
I break my bread to share with you.

In God's new world we share the Bread of Life.

As women shed their blood to give you life,
I shed my blood to give you a new life.

In God's new world we share the Wine of Heaven.

COME, LET us celebrate the supper of Jesus.
Let us make a huge loaf of bread and let us bring
abundant wine.

Because today we celebrate our meeting with Jesus.
Today we renew our commitment to the kingdom.
Nobody will be hungry.

WHEN WE break bread together,
do we not share in the Body of Christ?

We seek to share your life, gracious God.

When we take the cup,
do we not share in the life-blood of Christ?

We seek to share your life, gracious God.

Be present, be present,
even though we are unworthy for you to come
to us.
Only your peaceful presence
can nourish us in faith,
bind us together in love
and fill us with hope.
So that we might share in your service. Amen.

As we have shared our hopes and prayers and concerns,
we now share bread and wine together
as a symbol of God's presence among us and within us . . .
as a symbol of the Spirit who works through us . . .
Let us offer ourselves and all our struggling,
the needs we have expressed
for ourselves and for others
and for all those whose needs are beyond our knowing . . .
Let us offer our lives
with all our hopes and fears, attempts and failures –
that we may find hope and strength
and glimpse something of the life-giving energy of love,
and be nourished.

Bread   BROKEN for us

Wine   Poured out for us

Christ   Dying and living for us.

O LIVING Bread from Heaven,
Jesu, our Saviour good,
who your own self hast given
to be our soul's true food.
For us your body broken
hung on the cross of shame.
This bread is hallowed token
we break in your true name.

O Stream of Love Unending
poured from the one true Vine,
with our weak nature blending
the strength of life divine.
Our thankful faith confessing
in thy life-blood outpoured.
We drink this cup of blessing
and praise your name, O Lord.

Today we share bread and wine together
as a sign that we are one humanity,
as a pledge that we will work for justice,
as a foretaste of that which can be
despite what is and what has been.
May the Holy Spirit that guides us all
be present in this feast,
taking this bread and wine,
the concerns that we have expressed,
the lives that we lead,
and transforming them all
for the unity of humankind
and the service of love.

Blessed be the Eternal Sustainer.
Working with soil and elements and human toil.
Bringing forth bread from the earth.

**When the bodies of others are broken,
we are broken.**

Blessed be the Eternal Sustainer.
Working with soil and elements and human toil.
Making the fruit of the vine.

**We are all one kin, one blood.
When the blood of others spills, our blood
is spilled.**

With bread and wine, the signs of God's passion,
 – let us celebrate the passion of God's own heart
 – let us remember the passion of the world
 – and let us offer the passion of our hearts.

The Eucharist

1 GOD IS with us.
Her Spirit is here.

Lift up your hearts.
We lift them up to God.

Let us give thanks to your Inspirator.
It is right to offer her thanks and praise.

Spirit of God, who breathes fire into our very existence, filling us with heavenly joy and holy indignation at the plight of our world. We worship you, we praise you, we recognize the symbol of your presence, your promise of solidarity with us on our journey.

We claim the sign of renewal given to a broken and discouraged community, now as then in Jerusalem.
For you came to your own, filling them with confidence, gusting through their lives, bringing ecstasy and wholeness, clarity and vision, hope and peace.
You enlightened their existence,
Enabled their mission,
Empowered them to be disciples of your word.

So, with all the women who followed you through your ministry, who watched you die and rise again,
and with all those who inspired and supported the early Church, with Tabitha who showed solidarity with the poor,
Lydia who welcomed the tired and travel weary
and Priscilla who knew the meaning of persecution,
we praise you, singing:

Holy, Holy,
God of all power!
Heaven and earth are full of your glory.
Come and deliver us, come and deliver us, come and deliver us,
God most high.

Blessed is One who comes in the name of our God!
Come and deliver us, come and deliver us, come and deliver us,
God most high.

Blessed is Christ our brother,
who fills us with a sense of being one people, one community.
On the night he was betrayed,
he took bread, gave thanks, and broke it, saying:
'This is my body, which is given for you. Do this to remember me.'
In the same way, after supper he took the cup, blessed it and said:
'This cup is the new covenant made in my blood.
Do this whenever you drink it to remember me.'

Christ has died.
Christ is risen.
Christ will come again.

As one community we rejoice in your gifts,
we accept responsibility for our world;
we trust in your Spirit of challenge;
we welcome your presence in this bread and wine.
Drunk with longing for your deep and disturbing presence to be
revealed to us, we praise you with all who have derived inspiration
from this story of renewal and refreshment.

Come now, pour your Spirit on us so we are better able to
proclaim your message,
see new visions,
dream new dreams.

In the name of Christ.

Through him, with him, in him,
In the unity of the Holy Spirit,
All honour and glory be given to you,
O God our Source and Inspiration,
Now and forever.
Amen.

Take and eat, for the peace of all nations.

Take and drink, for the love of all people.

For you have shown us the path that leads to life.
And this feast will fill us with joy.

2   Mᴀʏ ɢᴏᴅ be with you.
And also with you.

Lift up your hearts.
We lift them to our God.

Let us adore and exalt our God.
It is right to give our thanks and praise.

O Eternal Wisdom,
We praise you and give you thanks,
because the beauty of death could not contain you.
You broke forth from the comfort of the grave;
before you the stone was moved,
and the tomb of our world was opened wide.
For on this day you were raised in power
and revealed yourself to women
as a beloved stranger,
offering for the rituals of the dead
the terror of new life
and of desire fulfilled.

Therefore, with the woman who gave you birth,
the women who befriended you and fed you;
who argued with you and touched you;
the women who annointed you for death;
the women who met you, risen from the dead;
and with all your lovers throughout the ages,
we praise you, singing:

Holy, holy,
Holy, holy.

God of all power,
God of all power.

Heaven and earth are full of your glory,
Heaven and earth are full of your glory.

Come and deliver us, come and deliver us, come and deliver us,
God most high.
**Come and deliver us, come and deliver us, come and deliver us,
God most high.**

Blest is one who comes in the name of our God.
Blest is one who comes in the name of our God.

Come and deliver us, come and deliver us, come and deliver us,
God most high.
**Come and deliver us, come and deliver us, come and deliver us,
God most high.**

Blessed is our brother Jesus,
who walks with us the road of our grief,
and is known again in the breaking of bread;
who, on the night he was handed over,
took bread, gave thanks, broke it, and said:

'This is my body, which is for you.
Do this to remember me.'
In the same way also the cup, after supper, saying:
'This cup is the new covenant in my blood.
Do this whenever you drink it,
to remember me.'

**Christ has died.
Christ is risen.
Christ will come again.**

Come now, disturbing spirit of our God,
breathe on these bodily things
and make us one body in Christ.
Open our graves, unbind our eyes,
and name us here;
touch and heal all that has been buried in us,
that we need not cling to our pain,
but may go forth with power
to release resurrection in the world.

3 O GOD, our Father and our Mother
The God who is and was and will be
before and beyond our little lives.
Who made all that is.
And who is known to us in our own hearts
And in the lives of others.

We come once more to trace the pattern
of death and resurrection
that is written throughout our world.

With the saints and ancestors
we behold that mystery
and beholding it adore you.

(Singing) **Holy, Holy, God of all power.**
Heaven and earth are full of your glory.
Come and deliver us, come and deliver us, come and deliver us,
God most High.

Blessed is One who comes in the name of our God.
Come and deliver us, come and deliver us, come and deliver us,
God most High.

At Easter we are close to the agony of Good Friday.
To the terrible humiliation of Jesus.
Scourged and crucified;
mocked and driven out,
as your children are hurt and humiliated still.

Yet that same agony flowered in joy.
The flower grew in the dark of the tomb
and burst apart the rock.
In taking bread and wine,
touching, breaking, pouring, drinking,
we know that we enter the holiest mystery
and that by doing so our hearts will be changed.

Jesus, on the night of betrayal, took bread,
he gave thanks for it and broke it
and gave it to his friends, saying:
'Take and eat. This is my own body which
I surrender because of you.
Do the same action to remember me.'

Then, after supper, he picked up the cup of wine.
He gave thanks for that and passed it around,
saying, 'Everyone drink of this.
This is my blood witnessing to a new understanding;
I spill it for you and for many more to cure the
wounds of the spirit and to take away ignorance.
When you eat together, drink like this,
and remember what I say.'

At Easter, as at every Eucharist, we recall the days of
Jesus' Passion with wonder and love.
We ask you, God creator, to enter this action so that our
hearts are moved to loving, and our fear and spite fade away.
We only partly understand what we do, and we ask you to
fill out our intention to fulfil your divine purpose,
that all who partake of this Easter feast may be
completed in grace.

Glory be to you, and may a glimpse of that glory
be allowed to us.

President   *(Breaking the bread)*

In breaking this bread and sharing it
We share in the death of Jesus, the pain of the world,
the hope of resurrection.

All   **And by partaking we become one body.**

President   In pouring this wine and sharing it
We enter into the passion of Jesus,
the blood shed in the world,
and the hope of resurrection.

All   **By drinking we become one body.**

4   WE take bread
symbol of labour – exploited, degraded
symbol of life.

Life for us.

We will break the bread
because Christ the source of life
was broken for the exploited and downtrodden.

Broken for us.

We take wine
symbol of blood spilt in war and conflict
symbol of new life.

Poured out for us.

We will drink the wine
because Christ the peace of the world
was killed by violence.

Because of us.

Now bread and wine are before us;
the memory of our meals;
our working;
our talking;
our loving.
Before us the depths of our life.

Thanks be to God.

The Spirit of God be with you

And also with you.

Lift up your hearts.

We lift them up to God.

Let us give thanks to God.

It is right to offer thanks and praise.

We give thanks for the history of God's people;
the defiance of the prophet
in startling and angry tongue,
in lonely dispute
and long, tiring conflict.

Thanks be to God.

For Jesus of Nazareth
living the truth of God
and the truth of us.
Bringing good news to the poor,
liberation for the oppressed
and for all down the ages
who have lived Jesus' story.

Thanks be to God.

For the promptings of the Spirit.
For all we know of ourselves;
the story that shapes us,
the grieving and the pain,
the oppressor that lies deep in our own soul,
the seeking and the loving.

Thanks be to God.

For all that binds us together in our humanity,
with all who live and have lived,
who have cried and are crying,
who hunger and are thirsty,
who pine for justice
and who sing and pray for the coming of God's kingdom.

Holy, Holy,

Holy, Holy.

God of all power,

God of all power.

Heaven and earth are full of your glory,

Heaven and earth are full of your glory.

Come and deliver us, come and deliver us, come and deliver us,
God most High.

**Come and deliver us, come and deliver us, come and deliver us,
God most High.**

Blest is One who comes in the name of our God.

Blest is One who comes in the name of our God.

Come and deliver us, come and deliver us, come and deliver us,
God most High.

**Come and deliver us, come and deliver us, come and deliver us,
God most High.**

We are bound to each other
and with all people
regardless of sex, race or class.
And in this we are bound to Jesus
who, in the same night that he was handed over
to torture and execution
took bread and gave you thanks,
he broke it and gave it to his friends, saying:
Take, eat, this is my body, my living presence, given for you;
do this to re-member me.

In the same way he took the cup of wine
and gave you thanks and gave it to them, saying:
Drink this all of you; for this is my blood, my very life;
spent for you; do this to re-member me.

We eat this food to bring us together.
We drink this wine to bring us alive in the world.

This is the death we celebrate.
This is the new life we proclaim.
This is the vision we live.

So we are joined with all who labour for justice;
with all women and men of faith;
with all who share our love of Jesus,
and those who seek truth and liberty in different ways.
We live and grow together
and we keep alive the memory of Jesus and his cross.
We awaken our hope in the resurrection,
in the new life where injustice lies defeated.

Strengthen us, O God.

We pray together that in eating the bread
and drinking the wine
our life will be enriched
and we make, here and now,
the new age a reality.

Amen.

We break this bread recalling the body of Christ broken for us.

**Help us to accept the cost of discipleship
and to take the risk of faith.**

The bread and wine are shared amongst the community, with the words:

The body of Christ, broken for you.

The blood of Christ, shed for you.

5   LET US give thanks.

For all that is good.

Let us give thanks
for the continuity of the universe;
for the sun rising day by day,
and the moon rising night by night;
for all the life with which we share this planet;
for the interactions and connections that bind us to it,
and the elements of which all is composed.

Let us give thanks.

And seek to live in harmony with all about us.

Let us give thanks
for the flow of human history;
for the events that have shaped and moulded us
and all our sisters and brothers;
for those who question that history;
for those who unearth the stories of the vanquished,
the oppressed, the forgotten, the unrecorded.

Let us give thanks.

**And take our place in the human story,
struggling for the unity of humankind.**

Let us give thanks
for those who have provided inspiration and hope;
for prophets and martyrs and poets;
thinkers and preachers and healers;
for those who have linked thought and action;
for reformers and rebels and strikers.

Let us give thanks.

And join with them in the quest for justice.

Let us give thanks
for all who have revealed or discovered deep and lasting truths;
let us celebrate their lives and deaths,
their thoughts and writings,
their continuing witness in the world today.

Let us give thanks.

And share in spreading this prophetic vision.

Today we give thanks for Jesus of Nazareth,
in whom Christians believe that God was especially present,
one of the channels through which God was made known to
humanity.
On the night that he was betrayed, he feasted with his followers;
he took bread, gave thanks, broke it
and gave it to his disciples, saying,
'Take this and eat it.
This is my body broken for you.
Do this in remembrance of me.'

In the same way, after supper,
he took the cup of wine, gave thanks,
and gave it to them, saying,
'Drink from it all of you.
This is my blood of the new covenant,
poured out for you and for many.
Do this whenever you drink it
in remembrance of me.'

For all that Jesus of Nazareth means to us.

We give thanks.

So today we share bread and wine together
as a sign that we are one humanity,
as a pledge that we will work for justice,
as a foretaste of that which can be
despite what is and what has been.
May the Spirit that guides us all
be present in this feast,
taking this bread and wine,
the concerns that we have expressed,
the lives that we lead,
and transforming them all
for the unity of all creation
and the service of love.

**God, whose body is all creation,
may we come to know you in all the earth
and feel you in our blood.
So will no part of us, or the world,
be lost to your transforming grace.**

Alleluia! This living bread is broken
for the life of the world.

Alleluia! Let us keep the feast.

An Easter Eucharist

*For congregation, priest, and six or more voices, this complete service was
used with a congregation of about 40. It was more formal than most of
our services, with speakers we had rehearsed in advance. The idea was to
use the dramatic power of liturgy.*

President   THEY HAVE taken away the Lord, and we know not where they
have laid him.

1   The women came to the cross
To stay beside their dying friend
The women came to the cross.

2 The women stood
   Watching the pain that was unbearable
   The women stood.

3 The women held
   The broken body in their arms
   The women held.

4 The women dressed
   The wounded body in its bandages
   The women wept.

President Sir, they have taken away my Lord and I know not where they
   have laid him.

5 Mary.

President Rabboni.

1 The women saw
   The women looked upon the risen truth
   The women saw.

2 The women told
   They told the truth of Resurrection
   And they were not believed.

Pause

CONFESSION

Death is
fear, lies, hate, envy, avarice, greed, lust, pride, destructiveness,
violence, cruelty.

Save us from death.

Life is
love, truth, courage, laughter, giving, creativeness, tenderness,
humility, kindness.

Give us life.

Forgive us.

When we choose death instead of life.

Light us.

To life – the life of Jesus.

May God forgive us all
May we forgive ourselves
And one another.

GLORIA

All   We adore the glory and the truth that is God.
Everything within us utters praise.
Our being is formed for this purpose and no other.
All our loves and works find meaning in you.

Jesus, who shows us what God is like,
forgive us our failure to understand
but keep us in your dazzling presence.

For there we learn the nature of holiness
and partake with you in the secret of the godhead.

COLLECT

Jesus, who was lost and found in the garden
never to be lost again,
stand by us in the darkness of our crucifixions,
as the women stood by you.
Die and rise with us in the suffering of the world.
Be reborn with us
as love and hope and faith and endurance
outlast cruelty and death. Amen.

READINGS

Old Testament	Ezekiel 37.1–14
New Testament	1 Peter 1.3–9
Gospel	John 20.11–18.

Instead of a sermon four people will tell us briefly what Easter means to them.

HYMN

INTERCESSION

One by one, six people light a big candle. Between each request the congregation are invited to call out appropriate names.

1   I light this candle, this beam in the darkness, because it shines in the likeness of Christ.

2   I light this candle for all the dispossessed of the world – for refugees, for those who are stateless, homeless, imprisoned, tortured – that they may find Jesus is with them upon their cross.

3   I light this candle for the sick and the bereaved, that in their pain and darkness they may discern hope and resurrection.

4   I light this candle for all the hungry of the world, that they may be filled.

5   I light this candle for all those who, because of class, race or sex, feel unloved and unwanted. May they find love.

6   I light this candle for this Community, St Hilda's, which seeks a new love, a new justice, a new Christian awareness which will be resurrection for many.

All   **That the light of Christ be shed abroad in the world. Alleluia.**

THE PEACE

President   Let peace flow like a river.

The congregation exchanges the kiss of peace.
Baskets will be passed round for the offertory.

HYMN

OFFERTORY

President   We hold up our smallness to your greatness:
our fear to your love
our tiny act of giving to your great generosity
ourselves to you.

God be with you.

And with your spirit.

We turn our faces to God.

We offer our hearts.

EUCHARISTIC PRAYER

President   O God, our Father and our Mother.
The God who is and was and will be
before and beyond our little lives.
Who made all that is.
And who is known to us in our own hearts
And in the lives of others.

We come once more to trace the pattern
of death and resurrection
that is written throughout our world.

With the saints and ancestors
we behold that mystery
and beholding it adore you.

(Singing)   **Holy, Holy, God of all power**
Heaven and earth are full of your glory.
Come and deliver us, come and deliver us, come and deliver us,
God most High.

**Blessed is the One who comes in the name of our God.
Come and deliver us, come and deliver us, come and deliver us,
God most High.**

At Easter we are close to the agony of Good Friday.
To the terrible humiliation of Jesus.
'Scourged and crucified';
mocked and driven out,
as your children are hurt and humiliated still.

Yet that same agony flowered in joy.
The flower grew in the dark of the tomb
and burst apart the rock.
In taking bread and wine
touching, breaking, pouring, drinking,
we know that we enter the holiest mystery
and that by doing so our hearts will be changed.

Jesus, on the night of betrayal, took bread,
he gave thanks for it and broke it
and gave it to his friends, saying:
'Take and eat. This is my own body which
I surrender because of you.
Do the same action to remember me.'

Then, after supper, he picked up the cup of wine.
He gave thanks for that and passed it around,
saying: 'Everyone drink of this.
This is my blood witnessing to a new understanding;
I spill it for you and for many more to cure the
wounds of the spirit and to take away ignorance.
When you eat together, drink like this,
and remember what I say.'

At Easter, as at every Eucharist, we recall the days of Jesus'
Passion with wonder and love.
We ask you, God creator, to enter this action so that our hearts are
moved to loving, and our fear and spite fade away. We only partly
understand what we do, and we ask you to fill out our intention
to fulfil your divine purpose, that all who partake of this Easter
feast may be completed in grace.

Glory be to you, and may a glimpse of that glory be allowed to
us.

(Breaking the bread)

In breaking this bread and sharing it we share in the death of Jesus, the pain of the world, the hope of resurrection.

And by partaking we become one body.

(Pouring the wine)

In drinking this wine and sharing it we enter into the passion of Jesus, the blood shed in the world, and the hope of resurrection.

By drinking we become one body.

THE COMMUNION

During the distribution hymns will be sung.

All   God, who cares for us,
the wonder of whose presence fills us with awe.
Let kindness, love and justice shine in our world.
Let your secrets be known here as they are in heaven.
Give us the food and hope that we need for today.
Forgive us our wrongdoing
as we forgive the wrongs done to us.
Protect us from pride and from despair
and from the fear and hate which can swallow us up.
In you is truth, meaning, glory and power,
while worlds come and go. Amen.

President   Let us share our joy and our gratitude.

The congregation may clap, ring bells, throw streamers . . .

HYMN

THE BLESSING

President   The blessing of God, in all the manifestations of God, rest upon each of our heads this night and bring us joy and love and hope.
The blessing of Jesus, who showed us what love might be, enter each of our hearts.
The blessing of the Spirit, who gives renewed life and energy and wisdom, delight our spirits.

Go forth into the world and keep the faith. **Amen.**

A St Hilda's Day Celebration

WELCOME AND INTRODUCTION

ST HILDA READING

COLLECT

All   O GOD our vision,
in our mother's womb
you formed us for your glory.
As your servant Hilda
shone like a jewel in the Church,
may we now delight to claim her gifts
of judgement and inspiration
reflected in the women of this age,
through Jesus Christ. Amen.

DANCE

CONFESSION *(read sentence by sentence going round circle)*

We do not accept that it is right to exclude women from sharing
fully in the spiritual journey.
We confess that it is sometimes hard to stand beside those who
work for change.
We confess it is sometimes easier to deny the existence of
injustices.
Loving God, keep us strong in our intent to do what we know to
be right.

READING *('Sisters' by Wendy Cope)*

HYMN *('Praise to God, the World's Creator')*

PRAYER *(said sentence by sentence going round circle)*

We give thanks today
for St Hilda, a jewel amongst women,
for Mary, the first Apostle,
for Julian of Norwich,
and for all the women, known and unknown, who have brought
their own insights and gifts to the churches.
We acknowledge and praise them.

We give thanks today
for all women in society who have struggled for change, endured
contempt, suffered ill treatment, but who have stood firm in their
convictions.

We give thanks today
for all women who have nurtured and cared for us,
for all women who have challenged and entertained us through
writing, music and performance,
for friends and colleagues,
and for all women past and present who have inspired us and
helped us on our journey through life.
We remember and honour them.

(Naming of women – Lighting of candles)

READING *('Why Dorothy Wordsworth is not as Famous as her Brother')*
by Lynn Peters)

DANCE

READING *('Poem from Holloway Prison 1912' – Anonymous)*

THE PEACE *(From 'Living by the Word' by Alice Walker)*

Knock and the door shall be opened. Ask and you shall receive.
Whatsoever you do unto the least of these, you do also unto me –
and to yourself. For we are one. God answers prayers. Which is
another way of saying, 'the Universe responds'.

We are indeed the world. Only if we have reason to fear what
is in our own hearts need we fear for the planet. Teach
yourself peace.
Pass it on.

HYMN (*'Come celebrate the women'*)

All   As Christ shared bread and wine with his disciples,
so we bring bread and wine to share.
If I eat my bread with joy
and drink my wine with a merry heart
it is because I have seen Happiness,
have known Joy,
and know what I have seen and heard.
In the sharing of this bread and this wine
Let us remember and give thanks for the mystery of faith
and Christ's great gift of love and hope.

We pass the bread and wine, with the words:

The Bread of Love

The Wine of Hope

READING (*From 'Living by the Word' by Alice Walker*)

All-embracing God,
empower us with your love
enrich us with your grace
strengthen and protect us.

BLESSING

All   Let us go out in hope
with strength, courage and love.
Let us keep walking!

Post Communion

WHEN people turn
from the table
where bread is broken
and candles glow,
be sure you have invited them
not to your house
but to their own,
and offered not your wisdom
but your love.

LET US go out in peace and in power.
To love and serve the Lord.

THE FEAST is ended; depart in peace.
The work of the world lies before us.
Accomplish justice, with grace.

THOSE WHO work for change suffer resistance.

So make us strong.

Those who do new things sometimes feel afraid.

So make us brave.

Those who challenge the world as it is arouse anger.

So grant us inner peace.

Those who live joyfully are envied.

So make us generous.

Those who try to love encounter hate.

So make us steadfast in you.

Blessing

THE BLESSING of the God of Sarah and Hagar, as of Abraham.
The blessing of Jesus born of the woman Mary.
The blessing of the Holy Spirit who broods over us
as a mother over her children,
Be with us now and forever. Amen.

MAY THE power and the mystery go before us, to show us the way,
shine above us to lighten our world,
lie beneath us to bear us up,
walk with us and give us companionship,
and glow and flow within us to bring us joy. Amen.

MAY THE God who dances in creation,
who embraces us with human love,
who shakes our lives like thunder,
bless us and drive us out with power
to fill the world with her justice. Amen.

THE blessing of God,
The eternal goodwill of God,
The shalom of God,
The wildness and the warmth of God,
be among us and between us
Now and always. Amen.

MAY Holy Wisdom,
kind to humanity,
steadfast, sure and free,
the breath of the power of God;
may she who makes all things new, in every age,
enter our souls,
and make us friends of God,
through Jesus Christ. Amen.

NOW MAY every living being,
Young or old,
Living near or far,
Known to us or unknown,
Living, departed or yet to be born,
may every living being
be full of bliss. Amen.

Music

We use traditional hymns and carols, Taizé chants, and sometimes other chants (e.g. Peruvian) taught us by members. We are beginning to think about making up dances to music we particularly enjoy, but have not got very far in writing our own hymns.

RAGE, WISDOM, and our lives inflame
so living never rests the same:
you are creative power and art
to blow our mind and wrack our heart.

As fiery gale, as storm of love,
discomfort, burn, all wrong remove,
exposing with your searing light
the lovelessness we keep from sight.

Disrupt and right our unjust ways
With the abrasion of your grace,
while we're your foes let no rest come
till to Christ's love you've brought us home.

You gust and burn through time and space,
and strange your beauty, fierce your face;
disturb our sleep and break our peace;
till Christ's love win, don't, Lady, cease.

Bring us to love the Father, Son,
and you with them in love as one,
that through the ages all along
this may be our endless song:

Praise to love's eternal merit,
Father, Son and wisest Spirit.

vige, creatrix sophia
cordas tuorum inflamma
tu artis vis et studiae,
mentium es turbatio.

ventus amoris ignifer
mala combure omnia;
lumen adurens eluce
nostra detegens odia.

rumpe omnem iniuriam
asperitate gratiae;
dum hostes sumus oppugna
donec nos Christo tradamur.

pulchra tu fera domina,
et flas ubique flagranter;
somnum et pacem deportans
Christi nos implens amore.

doce nos te agnoscere
cum patri et cum filio
in caritate coniunctam
et nobis delectatio.

JUBILATE Deo, Jubilate Deo, Alleluia.

YOU CAN'T kill the spirit
She is like a mountain
Old and strong
She goes on and on.

O LORD, hear my prayer, O Lord hear my prayer;
When I call answer me.
O Lord hear my prayer, O Lord hear my prayer;
Come and listen to me.

UBI caritas et amor
Ubi caritas
Deus ibi est.

BLESS the Lord, my soul,
and bless his holy name.
Bless the Lord, my soul,
he leads me into life.

YOU SHALL go out with joy
and be led forth with peace,
and the mountains and the hills shall break forth before you.
There will be shouts of joy
and the trees of the field
shall clap, shall clap their hands.

And the trees of the field shall clap their hands,
and the trees of the field shall clap their hands,
and the trees of the field shall clap their hands,
and you'll go out with joy.

For all the saints who from their labours rest,
Who in the world their faith in God confessed,
Your name, O Jesus, be forever blessed.
Alleluia! Alleluia!

You were the Stranger in the dark of night,
With whom they strove to find their one true light,
To whom you gave God's blessing, ever bright.
Alleluia! Alleluia!

They are the folk who gave with love divine,
Always in service did their wills incline,
Forgetting self, they did with glory shine.
Alleluia! Alleluia!

They followed you, cast out the city's gate,
Killed by the eyes and guns of human hate,
Yet trumpets sound their resurrection fête.
Alleluia! Alleluia!

And there will dawn a yet more marvellous day,
The saints with laughter sing and dance and play,
The Clown of Glory tumbles in the Way.
Alleluia! Alleluia!

Final Prayer

WE DO NOT understand, eternal God,
the ways of your Spirit in the lives
of women and men.
She comes along secret paths to
take us unawares.
She touches us in joy and sorrow
to make us whole.
She hides behind coincidence to
lead us forward and
uses our human accidents as occasions
for influence.
We do not understand but
we welcome her presence and
rejoice in her power.

Index